Pom-Pom's Big Win

Pom-Pom's Big Win
© 1999 Creative Teaching Press, Inc.
Written by Margaret Allen, Ph.D.
Illustrated by Priscilla Burris
Project Director: Luella Connelly
Editor: Joel Kupperstein
Art Director: Tom Cochrane

Published in the United States of America by:
Creative Teaching Press, Inc.
P.O. Box 6017
Cypress, CA 90630-0017

CTP 2904

Today is Pom-Pom's big day.
Pom-Pom sits on Jan's lap.

2

The man puts tags on the cats.

3

Pom-Pom is a big cat.
The man puts a tag on Pom-Pom.

Mom and Jan sit.

The man gets Kip.
The man pets Kip.
Kip sits.

The man has a cat toy.
Kip hits it.

7

The man has a toy rat.
Kip sits. Kip sits and sits.

The man gets Pom-Pom.
The man pets Pom-Pom.
Pom-Pom sits.

The man has a cat toy.
Pom-Pom hits it.

The man has a toy rat.
Pom-Pom spins. Pom-Pom spins and spins.

11

Pom-Pom wins!
The man puts a blue ribbon on Pom-Pom.
Pom-Pom, you win! You win!

Mom and Jan grin.
It is Pom-Pom's big day!

Mom and Jan grin and grin.

Pom-Pom naps on Jan's lap.

BOOK 4: Pom-Pom's Big Win

Focus Skills: w, k, short i

Focus-Skill Words		Sight Words	Story Words
win	is	day	blue
wins	it	gets	pets
Kip	sit	you	ribbon
big	sits		today
grin	spins		toy
hits			

Focus-Skill Words contain a new skill or sound introduced in this book.

Sight Words are among the most common words encountered in the English language (appearing in this book for the first time in the series).

Story Words appear for the first time in this book and are included to add flavor and interest to the story. They may or may not be decodable.

Interactive Reading Idea

Have your young reader practice reading words ending with *s*. Write *win, grin, hit, sit,* and *spin* in a column on a piece of paper. On another piece of paper, write the letter *s* five times in a column. Match the *s* sheet to the word sheet and have your young reader read the list again. What happens? *Win* becomes *wins. Grin* becomes *grins,* and so on.

16